Angela

James Moloney

Teacher's Guide
by Peter Bruck

Ernst Klett Verlag
Stuttgart Düsseldorf Leipzig

Dieses Lehrerheft bezieht sich auf die im Ernst Klett Verlag
erschienene Textausgabe von *Angela*, Klettbuch 57816.

Herausgegeben von Professor Dr. Peter Bruck, Lüdinghausen.

Verweise auf das Schülerbuch werden in Kurzform angegeben:
25,33 = Seite 25, Zeile 33.

1. Auflage   A 1 ^{5} ^{4} ^{3} ^{2} ^{1} | 2006 05 04 03 02

Die letzte Zahl bezeichnet das Jahr dieses Druckes.
© für diese Ausgabe Ernst Klett Verlag GmbH, Stuttgart 2002.
Internetadresse: http://www.klett-verlag.de

Redaktion: Katherine Inglis-Meyer M.A.

Umschlag: Sabine Frank, Stuttgart.
Fotos von Bobbi-Jo Brady und Emily:
Peter Evans, Alderley, Qld., Australia.
Druck: Gutmann + Co. GmbH, Talheim.
Printed in Germany.
ISBN 3-12-578161-2

Contents

1. James Moloneys *Angela* als interkultureller 4
   Unterrichtstext
2. Die didaktische Konzeption 7
3. Zur Anlage des Lehrerbandes 9
4. Getting the Course Started 10
5. First Teaching Unit: Section 1 of "Schoolies" 12
6. Second Teaching Unit: "Schoolies" 14
7. Third Teaching Unit: Angela and Gracey –
   the development of their friendship 17
8. Fourth Teaching Unit: Angela as the first-person narrator .. 21
9. Fifth Teaching Unit: Gracey's growing awareness of race ... 25
10. Sixth Teaching Unit: The issue of the stolen generation 28
11. Seventh Teaching Unit: Angela and Jarred 33
12. Worksheets and Skills Files 36
13. Post-reading Activities 42
14. Working with the Additional Texts 43
15. Suggested Tests 47

Useful Internet Addresses 55

1. James Moloneys *Angela* als interkultureller Unterrichtstext

In seiner Romantrilogie *Dougy* (1993), *Gracey* (1994) und *Angela* (1998) thematisiert der australische Jugendbuchautor James Moloney grundlegende Fragen des australischen Selbstverständnisses, die um die gegenwärtigen Beziehungen zwischen Anglo-Australiern und den *Aborigines* kreisen. In *Dougy* beschreibt Moloney, wie die schwarze Gracey als begabte Leichtathletin entdeckt wird und schließlich die "Queensland State Championship" in Brisbane in der 100-Meter Disziplin gewinnt. Der Roman beschreibt ferner die Auseinandersetzungen zwischen Weißen und Schwarzen und wirft anhand eines Stipendiumsangebotes an Gracey für den Besuch einer (weißen) Internatsschule die grundlegende Frage nach dem Verhältnis von individuellen und kollektiven Identitätsbildern auf. Gracey möchte zunächst ihre vertraute Umgebung nicht verlassen, weil sie befürchtet, auf einer weißen Internatsschule zu einer Weißen zu werden.

Zu Beginn des Romans *Gracey* besucht die Protagonistin als einzige Aborigine das weiße Hamilton College. Im Mittelpunkt der Darstellung steht die Entdeckung der eigenen Geschichte als Aborigine und deren Verfälschung durch die Anglo-Australier. Gleichzeitig zeigt der Roman die wachsende Entfremdung Graceys von ihrem ursprünglichen ethnischen Leben. Der Konflikt zwischen dem Anspruch der *Aborigines* auf eine ethnozentrische Lebensgestaltung und Graceys Anspruch auf Emanzipation und Selbstverwirklichung bleibt in dem zweiten Roman ungelöst. Moloney lässt seine Protagonistin nach Hamilton College zurückkehren. Dort will Gracey ihren Schulabschluss machen, um anschließend Jura studieren zu können.

Der dritte Roman, der aus der Perspektive der 17-jährigen weißen Angela erzählt wird, beginnt mit der Schulentlassungsfeier und endet mit der vorläufigen Trennung der beiden Freundinnen Angela und Gracey etwa ein Jahr später. Das Handlungsgeschehen vollzieht sich auf zwei Ebenen: einer persönlichen und einer inter-ethnischen. Die Ich-Erzählerin berichtet von ihrer Freundschaft zu Gracey und dem eigenen schmerzhaften Lernprozess, der die Erkenntnis einschließt, unbewusst und ungewollt eine rassistische Einstellung gegenüber den *Aborigines* zu haben. Sie beschreibt ferner Graceys wachsende ethnozentrische Orientierung sowie das allmähliche Auseinanderdriften der beiderseitigen Beziehung, und sie thematisiert die Freundschaft mit Jarred, einem Sportstudenten.

Auf der inter-ethnischen Ebene thematisiert der Roman die für die Schwarzen traumatische Erfahrung der *stolen generation*. Damit ist jener Vorgang angesprochen, durch welchen den *Aborigines* ihre Kinder durch weiße Behörden weggenommen und von Weißen erzogen wurden. Angela erfährt von der schuldhaften Verstrickung ihres Großvaters in dieses Unrecht und lernt so einen wesentlichen Aspekt des australischen Selbstverständnisses neu zu bewerten.

Angela ist zwar die Fortsetzung des Romans *Gracey*, ist aber ohne Bezug auf den zweiten Teil der Trilogie bzw. ohne jegliche Kenntnis dieses Teiles absolut verständlich. Überhaupt gilt, dass jeder Roman der Trilogie ohne weiteres aus sich heraus verstanden werden kann. *Angela* ist ferner ohne genaue Kenntnisse über die australische Gesellschaft und deren Geschichte verständlich, da etwa die Thematik der 'gestohlenen Kinder' im Roman selbst didaktisch entfaltet wird und der Leser Angelas eigenen Erkenntnisprozess begleitet. Dessen ungeachtet gewinnt der Roman einen besonderen interkulturellen Stellenwert, da sich an ihm exemplarisch aktuelle Probleme multikultureller Gesellschaften aufzeigen lassen. Im vorliegenden Fall betreffen diese die Entdeckung eines eigenen ethnischen Bewusstseins, die damit verbundene Dissimilation von der dominanten Mehrheitskultur sowie die Korrektur des weißen Selbst- und Weltverständnisses, aufgezeigt anhand der Bewusstseinsentwicklung von Angela.

Die Beschäftigung mit dem Roman vermag einen wesentlichen Bereich einer anglophonen Bezugskultur erschließen helfen. Darüber hinaus trägt die Auseinandersetzung mit einem Kernproblem der Bezugskultur dazu bei, Gemeinsamkeiten und Differenzen zwischen multikulturellen Gesellschaften zu entdecken und unter Einbeziehung der eigenen Lebenswirklichkeit kritisch zu befragen. Der Leser nimmt somit an dem sich verändernden australischen Selbstbild teil, indem er erfährt, wie der kulturell Andere sich selbst sieht und sein Selbstverständnis artikuliert. Dass *Angela* keine Patentlösung entwirft, sondern den Konflikt der beiden Freundinnen gerade auch nach deren schmerzhaften Lernprozessen unbewältigt lässt, unterstreicht einmal mehr die didaktische Relevanz dieses Jugendromans.

Die in *Angela* thematisierte interkulturelle Problematik lässt den Roman als besonders geeignet für fächerverbindendes Arbeiten auf der Jahrgangsstufe 12 erscheinen. Projektvorhaben wie z. B.

"Die Assimilations- und Dissimilationsproblematik in multikulturellen Gesellschaften" lassen sich unschwer mit dem Fach Sozialwissenschaften durchführen. Damit ist gleichzeitig der zweifache didaktische Standort des Romans innerhalb der Oberstufenarbeit angesprochen. Als Jugendroman, der schwerpunktmäßig als Beziehungsroman rezipiert wird, wird *Angela* auf der Jahrgangsstufe 11 zu lesen sein. Im Rahmen einer Unterrichtsreihe zum Thema *multicultural Australia* würde *Angela* hingegen auf der Jahrgangsstufe 12 gelesen. In diesem Fall würde die Freundschaftsthematik durch solche Aspekte wie Assimilation und Dissimilation vertieft und in den angesprochenen multikulturellen Kontext eingebettet.

Neben den angesprochenen interkulturellen Wissensfeldern bringt die Lektüre des Romans den wünschenswerten Umstand mit sich, dass der schulische Leser sensibilisiert wird für die Existenz unterschiedlicher '*Englishes*'. Die zahlreichen *Australianisms*, die in den Annotationen als solche gekennzeichnet wurden, machen ihn mit der Tatsache vertraut, dass es neben der ihm bekannten Unterscheidung von britischem und amerikanischem Englisch weitere zielsprachliche Sprachvarianten gibt. Die Beschäftigung mit *Angela* leistet damit abschließend auch einen wichtigen Beitrag zu der Bewusstseinsbildung über die sprachliche Vielfalt des Englischen als Weltsprache.

2. Die didaktische Konzeption

Literatur- und Textdidaktik stellen mittlerweile ein breites Spektrum unterrichtsmethodischer Zugriffe bereit, die hinlänglich bekannt sind und deren Begründungen nicht eigens entfaltet zu werden brauchen. Gleichwohl gilt es, die Voraussetzungen und Zielsetzungen des nachfolgend vorgestellten Unterrichtsmodells darzulegen.

Handlungsaufbau und Spannungsführung des chronologisch angelegten Romans legen ein sukzessives Vorgehen nahe. Der Text besteht aus sechs Teilen. Abschnitt 1 (SB **5**–15) des ersten Teiles "Schoolies" wird gemeinsam im Rahmen einer Doppelstunde gelesen und besprochen. Diese Erstbegegnung mit dem Text hat im wesentlichen einführende Funktion. Anhand einer Karte von Australien wird der geographische Handlungsschauplatz lokalisiert. Aspekte des kulturellen Handlungsortes – ein exklusives Mädcheninternat – werden gleichfalls angesprochen und erste Leseeindrücke zu den beiden Abiturientinnen gesammelt. Ferner werden Überlegungen zu der Art des Erzählvorganges sowie zu dem familiären Hintergrund der schwarzen Gracey angestellt.

Der restliche Teil von "Schoolies" (SB **15**–35) wird dann in häuslicher Vorbereitung gelesen, Worksheet I (s. S. 36) wird lektürebegleitend bearbeitet. Nach der Auswertung im Unterricht werden für bestimmte Schwerpunktthemen (cf. Worksheet II, S. 37) Zuständigkeiten festgelegt. Damit ist der weitere Leseprozess fokussiert; der Unterricht selbst wird von den zuständigen Schülergruppen eigenverantwortlich gestaltet. Präzisierungen und Ergänzungen werden im weiteren Unterrichtsverlauf vom Lehrer dort eingebracht, wo dies angezeigt ist.

Die Besprechung des ersten Teiles ist noch überwiegend lehrerzentriert und fragend-entwickelnd angelegt. Die Lerngruppe übt sich in der Anwendung textanalytischer Verfahren. Informationen zu den einzelnen auf dem Arbeitsblatt (Worksheet I) angegebenen Punkten werden zusammengetragen und ausgewertet.

Ein wesentlicher Aspekt ist in diesem Zusammenhang die Spracharbeit. Die Schülerinnen und Schüler sind hier gehalten, ihre lexikalischen Defizite zu benennen; im Unterricht selbst werden diese Ausdrucksmängel, die in der Regel das abstrahierende Auswerten von Informationen betreffen, gemeinsam abgebaut. Der sprachliche Lernzuwachs wird auf Folie oder an der Tafel fixiert.

Neben der Spracharbeit kommt der Schulung des Leseverständnisses große Bedeutung zu. Insbesondere auf der Jahrgangsstufe 11 werden Verarbeitungsformen des extensiven Lesens ggf. eingeführt oder vertieft werden müssen. Skill File 1, "How to read without a dictionary" (S. 38 –39), sollte den Schülerinnen und Schülern an die Hand gegeben werden, u. U. ist eine gesonderte Unterrichtsstunde zur Einführung und Schulung der Bedeutungserschließungsverfahren notwendig.

Die Beschäftigung mit den Teilen zwei bis sechs des Romans ist, wie bereits angesprochen, schülerzentriert. Im Gespräch gilt es zu klären, ob die Form der themenorientierten Gruppenarbeit durch kreative Schreibaufgaben zu ergänzen ist. Diese ergeben sich häufig an jenen Schnittstellen des Unterrichtsgesprächs, an denen kontroverse Einschätzungen etwa in Bezug auf die wachsende Entfremdung von Gracey und Angela auftreten. Das Verfassen von Tagebucheintragungen als Gracey und Angela oder als Jarred ist in solchen Zusammenhängen sinnvoll und vermag das Unterrichtsgespräch wesentlich zu befruchten.

Die hier vorgeschlagene Konzeption verlangt von den Kursteilnehmern ein hohes Maß an Arbeitsdisziplin und Verantwortung. Der Lehrer sollte ein bis zwei Doppelstunden für die Organisation der Gruppen, das Herausbilden gruppeninterner Zuständigkeiten und Verantwortlichkeiten zur Verfügung stellen. Um die Effektivität der Gruppenarbeit zu gewährleisten, hat es sich als zweckmäßig erwiesen, von den jeweiligen Gruppen Arbeitsprotokolle erstellen zu lassen. Diese sollten jeweils neben den Arbeitsergebnissen auch den Arbeits- bzw. Diskussionsprozess innerhalb der Gruppe aufzeigen. Damit ist eine doppelte Form der Rückmeldung gegeben. Die Gruppe selbst legt ständig Rechenschaft über ihren Arbeitsprozess ab, und der Lehrer ist stets über den jeweiligen Arbeitsstand informiert und kann erforderlichenfalls unterstützend eingreifen.

Neben der romanbezogenen Gruppenarbeit bietet *Angela* vielfältige Möglichkeiten textergänzender Arbeitsprojekte. Internetrecherchen zu Fragen der *Aborigines* usw. sind ergiebig und unterstützen das eigenverantwortliche Arbeiten. Die im Anhang angeführten Internetadressen bieten hierzu einen ersten Wegweiser. Weiterhin sollte die Möglichkeit von Internet-Chats ausprobiert werden. Interessierte Kursteilnehmer könnten versuchen, mit australischen Schülerinnen und Schülern Kontakt aufzunehmen oder aber ggf. beim Autor anfragen, ob dieser mit Anschriften von Schulen, in denen *Angela* gelesen wird, aushelfen kann. Darüber hinaus lässt sich auch mittels der im Anhang angegebenen deutschen Internetadresse ein entsprechender Gedankenaustausch herstellen. Insgesamt gilt, dass Einfallsreichtum und Beharrlichkeit viel versprechende Kontaktmöglichkeiten herstellen. Diese auszunutzen und fruchtbar zu machen sollte Motivation für jeden Kurs sein!

3. Zur Anlage des Lehrerbandes

Da das hier vorgestellte Unterrichtsmodell im Wesentlichen als projektbezogene Gruppenarbeit konzipiert ist, wurde auf eine Inhaltssynopse der Kapitel zwei bis sechs verzichtet. Stattdessen wird eine zusammenfassende Darstellung der jeweiligen Arbeitsprojekte vorgelegt. Diese Darstellung spiegelt gleichzeitig die erbrachten Schülerleistungen wider. Darüber hinaus werden weiterführende Impulse angeboten, mit denen die Textuntersuchung im Unterrichtsgespräch vertieft werden kann. Ergebnisfixierungen werden zu jeder Unit vorgestellt, so dass diejenigen, die eher lehrer- und unterrichtsbezogen arbeiten möchten, entsprechend verfahren können. Als Abschluss werden zwei Klausuren vorgeschlagen. Der erste Vorschlag, *Gracey at Hamilton College*, wendet sich in erster Linie an Schülerinnen und Schüler der Jahrgangsstufe 11, während der zweite Text, John Howards *Address to Corroboree 2000*, der zielsprachlich komplexer und inhaltlich deutlich anspruchsvoller ist, vor allem für die Jahrgangsstufen 12 und 13 geeignet ist. In beiden Fällen handelt es sich um fremde Texte, so dass unschwer die Unterrichtsreihe entsprechend abgeschlossen werden kann.

4. Getting the Course Started

The first section (SB **5–15**) of the first chapter, "Schoolies", can be read and discussed extensively in class (and tips given on the techniques of extensive reading, cf. Skills File 1). The rest of the chapter could then be read at home and Worksheet I filled in. The students' findings should be discussed together in the next lesson before they read the rest of the novel on their own at home. The teacher then presents the organisational plan of the course work and suggests the following procedure. 'While-reading' tasks (cf. Worksheet II) covering the reading process of the whole novel are handed out. After reading the entire novel students should decide which of the five topics they would like to pursue in detail and then sign up for it. These topics will be dealt with as projects. Some of the students are asked to keep a reading journal (cf. Skills File 2). They are informed that such a journal helps them to keep track of what they have read and to become more aware of their reactions to what they read. They are also told that the teacher will refer to these comments occasionally in class at appropriate moments.

Whereas the novel-based project work is obligatory, the project involving writing a screenplay is optional (cf. Skills File 3). Students should sign up for the project they are most interested in after they have read the novel.

The **structure of the course** thus looks as follows:

Classroom discussion and analysis of SB **5–15**
Chapter 1: "Schoolies". Reading time: two days
Reading time (whole novel): two weeks

Course work	approach
Comprehension; text analysis: evaluation of 'while-reading' tasks	teacher-based
Project organisation	teacher-based
Novel-based project work	student-centred

continued on next page

Presentation of project work	student-centred
1. Angela and Gracey: the development of their friendship.	
2. Angela as the first-person narrator	student-centred
3. Gracey's growing awareness of race	teacher-based
4. The issue of the stolen generation	
5. Angela and Jarred	
Presentation of optional project work	student-centred
Working with the additional texts (Student's Book)	teacher-based

The teacher could allow one or two ninety-minute periods for the preparation of the novel-based project work. Students can organise their group work with the help of these tips:

- Keep minutes of each group session. Your minutes should reflect your work process.
- Allocate areas of responsibility to members of the group (e.g. who's doing the minutes)
- Collect your material (e.g. relevant quotes)
- Analyse your material
- Present your findings to the course / class
- Hand in your project work to your teacher in a printed folder.

Naturally, students will need additional time to complete their work. This, however, should be done outside the regular English lessons.

5. First Teaching Unit: Section 1 of "Schoolies"

Synopsis

The first ten pages of *Angela* are read together in class as an introduction to the novel. In these pages the geographical and cultural setting as well as the two protagonists, Gracey, an Aboriginal girl, and Angela, who is white, are introduced. In addition, one major problem the novel deals with is also hinted at: Gracey's ethnic background and the difficulties she faces in the white world. "Schoolies" is set in Hamilton College, an exclusive all girls' boarding as well as day school in Brisbane, Australia. The first section depicts the girls' graduation day. The ceremony is about to begin when Angela, the first-person narrator, realises that her black friend, Gracey, is missing. Together with her mother, Cheryl Riley, Angela goes looking for her friend, who, as it turns out, does not feel up to attending the ceremony. She feels emotionally drained, having lost her mother and her brother Raymond the previous year. Thus she is all alone, nobody from her family being there to see her graduate.

The dialogue between these three characters clearly has the function of an exposition. To the reader unfamiliar with the two preceding novels, *Dougy* and *Gracey*, Gracey's background as well as her precarious position as the only Aboriginal in an exclusive white school are established. In addition, we are made aware of the close relationship between the two girls and their respective roles. Angela, who comes from a well-to-do Anglo-Australian, middle-class family, is portrayed here as the stronger person who displays initiative and resourcefulness, whereas Gracey seems to be somewhat helpless and lost. These roles will change later in the novel when Gracey starts to assert her ethnicity.

Teaching Steps

After the reading, the following questions are dealt with:
- *In which part of Australia is the novel set? Take a look at the map.*
- *What kind of school is Hamilton College? How does it seem to differ from German schools?*

- *What kind of narrator have we got here? What does this type of narration imply?*
- *Why does Gracey not want to attend the graduation ceremony?*
- *Which conflicts are already hinted at?*

The following answers can be expected:

Angela is set in Brisbane, Queensland; Hamilton College is an exclusive boarding and day school for girls. Except for Gracey there are no Aborigines there.

It differs from German schools in that even though it is non-denominational, it is not co-educational and virtually excludes the native part of the population. It is obviously private, i.e. fee-paying, and many of the girls are boarders and sleep in a dormitory. The pupils wear uniforms too, as in Britain, and have a graduation day to which parents and friends are invited, as in the USA.

The novel is narrated by Angela in the first-person, so we see everything from her point of view.

Gracey does not want to attend the graduation ceremony as she is the only graduate not to have her family there. Her mother as well as her brother Raymond died while she was at Hamilton College.

The difficulties of an Aboriginal in a predominantly white society are already hinted at through Gracey's position at the school and the struggle it was for her to reach graduation.

6. Second Teaching Unit: "Schoolies"

Synopsis

Even though Gracey has been attending a white college, she has retained close ties with her family. In fact, she is very family-minded and feels the need to be with her younger brother Dougy. So she leaves the school after graduation and returns to her home town, Cunningham.

After Christmas the Rileys spend their family vacation at the beach in Noosa. It is there that Angela receives a desperate phone call from Gracey who asks if she could stay with them. After Gracey's arrival Angela learns about her friend's growing estrangement from aboriginal life as Gracey confesses: "'... I don't think like them any more'" (**25**,33). Angela offers her emotional assistance, saying: "'You don't need to be lonely, Grace. You've got me and my family. You're a part of us now. We could almost be sisters. More like twins really'" (**27**,33–35). (She doesn't realize at this stage, of course, how condescending and naive she is being.)

The first chapter closes in a carefree and joyful atmosphere. Both girls have been accepted by the University of Queensland and are looking forward to their first year as university students.

Teaching Steps

First Step: Comprehension

1. *Why do Angela and Gracey part after one day of 'schoolies'?*
   Gracey has been invited to a special training camp for athletes and she also wants to spend Christmas with her younger brother, Dougy.

2. *What do we learn about the reasons for Gracey suddenly wanting to leave her home town and be with Angela again?*
   While in her home town Gracey painfully comes to realize that she no longer feels at home among her Aboriginal relatives. She feels lonely and out of place.

3. *What does Gracey mean when she tells Angela that she doesn't think like her relatives any more?*

She has grown away from the Aboriginal way of thinking and from Aboriginal values. Her education at a 'white' school has made her adopt the norms and values of Anglo-Australian society.

4. *Which courses at the University of Queensland have been offered to Gracey and Angela?*
Gracey has been offered a place in the course for Bachelor of Law and Angela in Human Resource Management.

5. *How would you describe the atmosphere at Noosa?*
The atmosphere is relaxed, easy-going and carefree.

Second Step: Evaluation of the reading assignment (→ Worksheet I)

Angela: from a white middle-class family; seems superficial, naive and fun-loving; seems to be racially unbiased; helps Gracey to assimilate into white middle-class society; is possessive and unconsciously patronizes Gracey

Gracey: is restless, seems to have no sense of belonging; estranged from her relatives; unsure about her identity; lonely, dissatisfied with her present situation

Their friendship: confidantes; Angela is the planner; she seems emotionally dependent on Gracey; like sisters: there's an intimate understanding and acceptance of the other

Angela's mother: understanding, outspoken; practical, persuasive, spontaneous; not bossy; unobtrusive with her advice

The race issue: There is no overt / open racism with the exception of one incident at Hamilton that happened in the past; there is latent racism: Angela, for example, does not seem able to accept ways of thinking and living that are different from hers; contrasting family structures: tribal vs. white middle-class norms, e.g. tribe: shared, communal responsibility for children; Angela and Gracey ignore their racial differences

The importance of family ties:	Gracey feels she has no family except Dougy; she needs to define the meaning of her people to her; her relatives do not understand her way of life; Angela takes traditional family values for granted; she is unaware of Gracey's problems or does not understand them
Angela as the first-person narrator:	"I" as a participant observer, restricted view; Angela evaluates everything Gracey does according to her own norms; we only occasionally receive insight into Gracey's feelings / state of mind

7. Third Teaching Unit: Angela and Gracey – the development of their friendship

The initial analysis of the first chapter has made the students aware of the fact that Angela and Gracey are very close friends who completely trust each other. The students might also have recognized the latent racism that characterizes Angela's attitude, although she herself is unaware of it. In addition to the insights gained from discussing the first chapter together in class, the students should realize two important points. Angela obviously can't imagine going to university without Gracey and so she always talks about their common future (cf.**18**,6ff.) and makes plans for them both. Even though Angela seems to be the stronger of the two, Gracey is definitely more mature because of her ethnic background and her experience of death in her family. While Gracey has experienced suffering and sorrow, Angela, by contrast, only knows the sheltered life of a white, upper middle-class girl.

Their relationship gradually changes after they have enrolled at the University of Queensland. Gracey meets a group of Aboriginal students on the campus who offer her help and support. At first Gracey is not really interested because Angela is always at her side, but later she gets more involved with this group, the "Indigenous Students Support Unit".

The two friends usually meet at "The Corner", a small cafe on the campus. One day Gracey is late for their regular meeting. When she finally arrives she tells Angela excitedly what it was like to have been with people of her own origin: "'I never realised what I was missing, Angela. Just to be with other people who ... who look like me for a start'" (**46**,14–15). From Angela's reaction ("'I didn't think that mattered to you anymore'" – **46**,17), we can conclude two things. She is obviously jealous as she is about to lose her 'monopoly' on Gracey and, moreover, she is, without realizing it, racist, as she seems to imply that Gracey had successfully separated herself from her ethnic background and that this separation was a good thing.

The first strain on their relationship occurs when Angela realizes that there is a part of Gracey's life from which she is excluded (cf. **48**,9–10). It begins to dawn on her that she is no longer the only important person in Gracey's life. She hides her feelings from Gracey, however, and lies about her thoughts on Rhonda Haines, the Aboriginal activist, in order not to hurt Gracey's feelings.

As Gracey is increasingly drawn into the ethno-political world of Rhonda Haines, she decides to move out of the Rileys' house and into a house rented by Aboriginal (Murri) girls. She defends her decision by stressing her desire for more contact with her own ethnic group: "'It's being round other black kids. Ever since I went to the Unit, I've felt so much better about being here. [...] It's feeling at home, being with a mob who pick up the same things as me'" (**60**,15–21). To Angela this comes as a complete surprise as she has never thought about Gracey in these terms and she is unable to grasp the significance that lies behind her friend's decision: "'I thought you didn't notice things like that anymore'" (**60**,22).

The growing estrangement between the two friends is paralleled by Gracey's growing sense of being a Murri. As she discovers the significance of her racial heritage, she gradually frees herself from Angela's dominating influence on her life. Angela, by contrast, is simply jealous, believing what is best for her is best for Gracey. As she confesses to her mother: "'I feel like I'm being slowly passed over for something better, [...] I'm being pushed out and it's not right. I'm better for Gracey than any of those others'" (**84**,27–37). What emerges here apart from her jealousy is Angela's racial superiority complex which ties in with her own latent racism.

Angela is confronted with her own racist attitudes when Gracey, who feels deeply hurt by her friend's patronizing attittude, bursts out: "'Generous to a fault as long as it's on your own terms. [...] It's all part of your power over me, isn't it? [...] You colonised me, Angela. From the day we met you moved in and started changing me'" (**96**,17–28). Even though Angela realizes that she has said the wrong things about Rhonda Haines ("It was the most reprehensible thing I had ever done" – **97**,28–29), she fails to see the racist implications of her own behaviour: "'Anything we've ever done was because we cared about you'" (**96**,33–34). Thus the two girls continue to grow apart, even though Angela tries to make amends.

Earlier mention was made of Angela's naiveté (cf. Second Teaching Unit) which is clearly one of the dominating traits of her personality.

While confronted with Gracey's growing ethnic self-awareness, Angela also undergoes a slow and painful discovery of her own racist view of blacks. When asked by Gracey: "'Tell me the truth, Angela. Do you like blacks?'" (**127**,22), Angela quickly replies: "'Yes, Gracey. Of course I do'" (**127**,25); she is still deceiving herself. Later, while discussing Gracey with her grandmother, she confesses: "'Grandma, I don't think I do like them [the blacks]. They ... well, it repels me. I don't know why'" (**157**,3–4).

This realization does not, however, make Angela accept Gracey's wish to return to her home town. As she tells her grandmother: "'I'd do anything to change Gracey's mind. [...]) I'd do anything to stop her'" (**157**,16–19). Only later, after she has learned about her grandfather's wrongdoings in the matter of the forced adoption of black babies by whites, does she begin to acknowledge her own racism. Remembering the words spoken by Gracey's brother Dougy ("'You think everything about you is better than everything about me'"), she realizes: "Dougy had seen into me deeply, in a way I could not see for myself" (**175**,30–32). Her new self-awareness finally enables Angela to accept Gracey on non-racist, unselfish and mature terms: "I realised too that I was glad of it, that I wanted her to be there [in Cunningham]. [...] Gracey was home and I was glad" (**184**,12–19).

Teaching Points

Depending on its thoroughness and depth, the students' report will probably have to be supplemented. The following task may be helpful.

Examine the following passages from the text and work out Angela's changing attitudes towards blacks:

46,17; **60**,13–37; **80**,11–14; **82**,23–30; **84**,36–37; **92**,22–**93**,4; **150**,33–**151**,6; **157**,7–19; **161**,25–28; **176**,1–16.

(Group work recommended.)

The students' report and the group work should yield the results as shown in the blackboard summary on the following page.

(Blackboard summary)

Angela and Gracey: the development of their friendship

- *initially*: mutual emotional dependence; confidantes; like sisters
- Angela enjoys being needed, enjoys her active role
- Angela ignores the racial differences and is unaware of her own latent racism
- Angela imposes her own standards and value system on Gracey
- Angela attempts to make Gracey like a white girl

- *later:* gradual estrangement because of Gracey's growing racial awareness
- Angela is jealous of Rhonda Haines
- she is made aware of her own racist attitudes
- she discovers her lack of ease with blacks
- she acknowledges her racial superiority complex
- she accepts Gracey as she is

➡ Angela has moved: – from innocence to experience
                                – from latent racism to an acceptance of ethnic identity

8. Fourth Teaching Unit: Angela as the first-person narrator

"No one knew Gracey better than me."

As the action is narrated by the 17-year-old Angela we have a first-person narrator as a participant-observer. As a participant, Angela narrates the events at Hamilton College and later at Queensland University, as well as in Sydney. In this role she relates the events as they concern her. Thus the focus of attention is on her own experiences and on her point of view. As an observer, by contrast, she also reflects on what is going on and makes judgements on both other people and her own behaviour.

Angela's role as a participant-observer makes for a reading process which allows the reader to be the critical judge of her reflections and evaluations. Hence as readers we are always forced to ask ourselves if Angela's observations, notably those on Gracey, are perceptive and/or reliable, or if she deludes herself into believing that she knows her friend properly.

When Gracey is faced with the graduation ceremony, which she believes she cannot cope with emotionally, Angela thinks: "No one knew Gracey better than me. *I* should have guessed" (**7**,19–20). She blames herself at this point for not having foreseen that Gracey might be emotionally overwrought because of the recent death of her mother and brother and the fact that no one from her family could be present. Angela is convinced that she can understand what Gracey is going through. Similarly when she concludes at the end of the ceremony that "Gracey had come through" (**15**,26), we are led to believe that she is a reliable interpreter of her friend's feelings. However, we are soon left wondering if Angela really is a competent interpreter of her friend's problems.

Consider the scene of Gracey's return from Cunningham, her home town. When she has related her estrangement from her family and the feeling of loneliness that goes with this experience, Angela only has this to say: "'You don't need to be lonely, Grace. You've got me and my family. You're part of us now. We could almost be sisters. More like twins really'" (**27**,33–35).

What emerges here is a mixture of naiveté and an unconsciously patronizing attitude. Angela, who does not really know or understand Aboriginal life, simply interprets the fact that she is Gracey's only friend to mean that she really knows her friend. Moreover, we gradually become aware that Angela views Gracey solely from her white upper-middle-class norms and actually disapproves of the Aborigines' way of life. For example, she cannot comprehend that within the value system of the tribal family structure of the Aborigines an early pregnancy is by no means a misfortune to be deplored. Instead she comments: "'That baby's mucked up her whole life'" (**26**,23f.).

The barrier of understanding becomes particularly clear when Gracey mentions to Angela the fact that her brother Dougy has "never seen the ocean" (**35**,18). When Angela responds by saying "'Bring him next year'" (**35**,26) and Gracey retorts: "'No, Angela, you don't understand what I'm getting at'" (**35**,28), we see that Angela's view is rather limited. Instinctively she realizes the barrier that exists between Gracey and herself but is unable to deal with it adequately: "I felt for a moment that nameless distance which sometimes fell between us" (**35**,31–33).

As the action progresses Angela's limited grasp of her friend's ethnic background becomes increasingly apparent. When Gracey tells her friend that she wants to live with other blacks Angela's lack of understanding is obvious: "And what was this about *after all those years at Hamilton*? Gracey had been happy there. If anyone knew that it was me" (**60**,35–37). Angela's blindness towards Gracey's need to be with other blacks stems, quite clearly, from her own racially motivated arrogance. Angela wrongly believes that she can determine if Gracey is happy better than Gracey herself ever could. And when Gracey reproaches her after Derek Campbell's speech on the stolen generation of not being able to understand her or any other black, she stresses Angela's naiveté: "'You! You don't know what grief is Angela. Not like Dougy and me or the people who spoke tonight […] You've never lost anybody close to you'" (**82**,13–16).

Significantly, Angela cannot understand what her friend has accused her of: "That was the second time she'd told me I couldn't understand as though I was blind …" (**82**,27–29). Her view does remain limited as long as she is racially biased. And it is only after she has admitted her prejudices to herself that she is able to truly accept Gracey as an Aboriginal.

Throughout the novel, Angela as a narrator who is a participant-observer retains her limited point of view. There are virtually no reflective passages in which she probes her own attitudes. Her occasional reflections show her to be shallow and superficial in racial matters but also deeply caring about her friend. As readers we literally accompany her on her mental and emotional journey towards an unbiased view of Aborigines. However, Moloney has obviously not wanted his adolescent readers to identify prematurely with Angela. There are a number of reported thoughts by the narrator presented to us from a retrospective point of view, as, for example, when she thinks: "I was too busy enjoying the sensation […] to pick up on her mood. I was going to pay for my negligence. Pay more than I could imagine" (**94**,31–33).

To the observant reader such phrases indicate that the author wanted there to be a certain amount of distance between his narrating heroine and the reader. (He also, of course, creates suspense this way.) It is precisely this detachment which constitutes the didactic value of Angela as the first-person narrator, making the reader, as it were, the critical judge of her thoughts.

Teaching Points

The analysis of the narrative structure and, in particular, of Angela as the first-person narrator often turns out to be the least popular subject among students. The students dealing with this task, therefore, may have to be given additional tips. These might include the following:

1. *Does the reader easily sympathize with Angela? If you think so, ask yourself if that sympathy remains the same throughout the novel.*
2. *If you think that the reader does not sympathize with Angela, work out why this is and how the author conveys this.*
3. *How reliable and perceptive are Angela's observations of Gracey?*

If the students' report turns out to be incomplete or needs supplementing, the following quotations from the novel could be examined in detail:

a) *"No one knew Gracey better than me."* (**7**,19)
b) *"That was the first time I heard the name* [Rhonda Haines]. *A name I was going to hear many times in the months ahead."* (**46**,27–28)

c) *"Gracey had been happy there* [at Hamilton]. *If anyone knew that, it was me."* (**60**,36–37)
d) *"I was too busy enjoying the sensation, the vibrancy of the place, to pick up on her mood. I was going to pay for my negligence. Pay more than I could imagine."* (**94**,31–33)
e) *"A handful of words but I regret them now as much as anything I have ever said."* (**95**,33–34)

Results to be expected from both the students' report as well as from the classroom analysis of the phrases above:

(Blackboard summary)

Angela as the first-person narrator

- Mode of narration: retrospective but never omniscient (limited knowledge of narrator)
- Angela as the narrator shares her information with the reader
- Angela is a biased participant-observer
- Angela's powers of reflection are clearly limited

Overall effect:

- reader witnesses and shares Angela's mental and emotional journey / development
- he / she becomes the critical judge of her opinions
- suspense is maintained

9. Fifth Teaching Unit: Gracey's growing awareness of race

"We're only alive while we're connected to our own people."

Just as Angela is to discover her latent racism and her prejudices about blacks, Gracey undergoes a profound identity crisis. In point of fact, the changes in Gracey's feelings about who she is may be read as a kind of journey towards the re-discovery and acceptance of her own roots.

Initially, Gracey is the well-adjusted boarding-school girl who has internalized white standards. Her assimilation is symbolically expressed by the change in her outward appearance. As Angela and Gracey recall: "'It still suits you, that bob. We had to do something with it. You still had your hair in a long plait, like a rope.' [...] 'I needed a complete make-over, didn't I? And you were just the person to do it'" (**13**,17ff.).

Inevitably, Gracey's assimilation into white, middle-class society causes problems with her own family and their way of life. Gracey has become rootless, she lives in a kind of ethnic and cultural no-man's land. As she puts it: "'... I'm back-packing through my whole life'" (**22**,21f.). Her estrangement from her own folks and the realization that she does not feel at home any longer in the town she comes from make her flee from Cunningham and seek shelter with Angela and her parents. As she confesses to her friend: "'I don't fit in because I don't think like them [her folks] anymore'" (**25**,33). Up to this stage, Gracey clearly displays a 'white' consciousness that sets her apart from her fellow blacks.

The gradual change in her ethnic self-awareness is reflected in her language. After she has started to spend time with other Aborigines on the university campus, Gracey begins to use the term 'Murri' instead of Aborigine (cf. **46**,11) and refers to other Murri kids as "our own" (**48**,7). Her growing awareness of race leads to a new orientation in her life. Gracey not only decides to move out of the Rileys' house, she also experiences a new feeling of what it means to be together with other blacks and develops a sense of racial belonging: "'Now I'm not alone anymore'" (**60**,24f.).

Gracey comes increasingly under the influence of black militant activist Rhonda Haines who serves as a racial and political mentor.

It is through being with Rhonda that Gracey sees herself as different from white society and begins to be proud to be a Murri: "'I'm so conscious of being a Murri that it hurts to think of the way I was'" (**126**,17f.).

Significantly, Moloney is not content with depicting his heroine's journey towards a new ethnic identity as ending with Gracey's new awareness of her own race. If this had been his intention, Gracey would have become a mere copy of Rhonda Haines, and *Angela* would be a completely political novel. Moloney, however, wants his heroine not only to become politically aware; he also wants her to become aware of her own ethnicity on her own terms. Thus Gracey's development from assimilation in white society to a disassociation from that society and a move towards her own ethnic group does not stop short at a militant Aboriginal stance on race. As Gracey confesses to Angela: "'... when I met Rhonda I started hating everything white and I fell into the trap, you see, that if everything white was wrong and bad then everything black must be good and right. Shit, was I naive'" (**127**,34–37).

Consequently, Gracey sets out to return to her roots. This time, however, she goes back to Cunningham as someone who has accepted her own blackness and wishes to start a new life from there: "'... I have to go back to Cunningham. To make sure I never forget I'm black, ever again'" (**150**,30–32). Gracey, who has reconciled herself to her black heritage, has finally come to realize that the meaning of life for her consists foremost of being with her own people: "'without a family that I feel part of, I'm not a Murri at all. That's where everything starts and finishes for me'" (**151**,4–6).

Teaching Points

The topic under discussion here is usually one that greatly motivates the students. Their reports, therefore, can be expected to present satisfactory results that will hardly need any supplementing by the teacher. However, in order to work out precisely the stages of Gracey's development, the class / course could be asked to study the following quotations, and trace Gracey's growing awareness of race:

- "*I needed a complete make-over, didn't I?*" (**13**,20)
- "*I thought I was over that. Hating Cunningham like I used to, before Mum died.*" (**25**,24f.)

- "[the Indigenous Student Support Unit] *is not my kind of thing really.*" (**44**,2)
- "*It's being around other black kids. Ever since I went to the Unit, I've felt so much better about being here.*" (**60**,15–17)
- "*I'm an Aborigine, Angela. My whole life is political.*" (**89**,19)
- "*There's stuff I never took any notice of, things about my people and where my land is. ... those things are more precious than a job or money ...*" (**151**,11–15)
- "*There's a life out there for me and I want to live it.*" (**152**,20f.)

The following results can be expected.

(Blackboard summary)

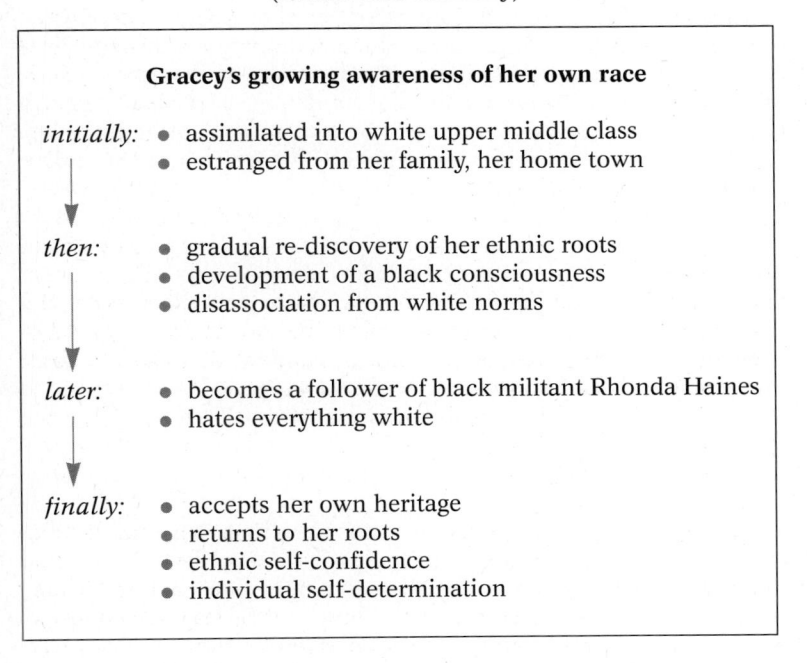

Gracey's growing awareness of her own race

initially:
- assimilated into white upper middle class
- estranged from her family, her home town

↓

then:
- gradual re-discovery of her ethnic roots
- development of a black consciousness
- disassociation from white norms

↓

later:
- becomes a follower of black militant Rhonda Haines
- hates everything white

↓

finally:
- accepts her own heritage
- returns to her roots
- ethnic self-confidence
- individual self-determination

10. Sixth Teaching Unit: The issue of the stolen generation

Undoubtedly, the issue of the stolen generation is one of the most controversial and sensitive domestic problems in contemporary Australia. The problem dates back to the early nineteenth century when the British Parliament sent missionaries to convert Aborigines to Christianity and appointed official Protectors who were to look after them and ensure that they learned to live within the white community. Subsequently, special 'protection laws' were introduced and the Aborigines were increasingly faced with severe restrictions on their way of living. With the passing of the Aborigines Protection Act in 1909 the government gained absolute authority over the daily lives of the Aboriginal peoples. That authority included the care, custody and education of Aboriginal children and the right to remove Aborigines at will from their homes or land. It was not until the late 1960s that the Aborigines were finally recognized as Australian citizens.

In *Angela*, the issue of the stolen generation is dealt with in an intricate way that is closely related to Angela's growing awareness of her true attitude towards blacks. She first learns about the issue when she attends a political rally with Gracey. There the topic is addressed by various speakers who all speak "of separation, of loss of family, of loss of country and of an overwhelming grief for what had been taken away" (**78**,8-10). Furthermore, Angela, and thus the reader, learns that the enforced separation from their Aboriginal home meant for the children a complete loss of their ethnic background and hence their identity. They were literally given a 'white' identity and, most notably, an English name.

Typically enough, Angela cannot grasp the existential, much less the political implications of the issue under discussion. To her mind, the individual biographies presented at the rally were only "moving" (**81**,29), as they displayed strong emotions. As Angela puts it: "'I heard those people speak about their grief. I know how it must feel'" (**82**,11f.). At this stage, it is beyond Angela's scope to recognize that the issue involves more than being moved or taken aback but is rather a question of fundamental human rights.

One of the speakers at the rally was a certain Derek Campbell who as a young boy had been separated from his mother. The driving force behind this case turns out to have been Angela's Grandpa Malvern, a retired pastor. So the issue takes on a personal note as Angela's family is directly involved.

Moloney has to be credited with having successfully managed to present the many facets of the problem from different points of view. Initially, Angela sympathizes with the ethnocentric white attitude imbued with liberal ideas as expressed by her mother: "'It wasn't all bad. Some of those kids were desperate. Taking them away saved their lives and gave them opportunities they would never have had'" (**88**,1ff.). The position formulated here is clearly utilitarian as it stipulates the belief that the end justifies the means. Moreover, it defends the government policy and works from the assumption of white supremacy, which chooses to neglect the Aborigine's humanity. Gracey's comment on Mrs Riley's views is here a case in point: "'I tell you, Angela, that story Cheryl told you doesn't make sense. For Murris, giving up your kid is like killing him. It's no different from plucking a leaf off a tree. We're only alive while we're connected to our own people'" (**129**,8–11). For a while, Angela is torn between her mother's view and Gracey's, her loyalty is divided as she feels she must defend her grandfather and, at the same time, she wants to placate an angry Gracey. It is only during a talk with a dinner guest of her grandparents that Angela finally learns the truth about the case of Derek Campbell and the role her grandfather played in it.

Harry Falkirk, a retired member of the Aboriginal Welfare Board and dinner guest at the Malverns', relates the true story of Derek Campbell's adoption to Angela. Describing the work of the AWB he notes: "'It was our job to see that half-caste kids like him could make the break, even if we had to twist a few arms to do it'" (**167**,9 f.). And he goes on to elaborate: "'I told her [Derek's mother] she had to let you have the oldest one or else we'd take away all three'" (**167**,24f.).

Three points are significant here. First, the 'gubba man' unintentionally confirms the earlier account by Derek Campbell himself and also Gracey's comment on the taking away of children. Thus Angela and the reader are made to realize that the mother was blackmailed into giving her oldest son away, that it was an enforced adoption. Secondly, Mr Malvern is forced to confront the fundamental illusion about his own part in this story, i.e. his conviction that the mother had given her son away voluntarily and that he had acted in the best interests of the boy. Thus he is forced to acknowledge his own guilt. This consisted in the fact that he lied to the white foster parents by telling them that Derek's mother had died in childbirth.

Third, the discussion reveals the motive governing Mr Malvern's action and which after all is also the driving force behind Angela's attitude towards Gracey. As Mrs Malvern pointedly puts it:
"'You were determined to kill off the black man in that Campbell boy, and to do it, you knew you had to cut him off from his family and his kind. [...] That's where the killing was, leaving all those half-dead people with their grief, longing to know what the other half of them meant'" (**174**,14–20).

Just as Angela's grandfather is made to think over his past actions towards blacks, Angela is forced to acknowledge her own white ethnocentrism that her grandmother confronts her with: "'... you despise what she [Gracey] comes from'" (**176**,4).

As Moloney has carefully refrained from writing a tendentious novel, the reader, especially the non-Australian reader, is left wondering about the impact of *Angela*. Here it may suffice to draw attention to the review reprinted in the Student's Book. There the reviewer states: "I found myself constantly wanting to take both sides in the conflict, but eventually reason dawned on me: it is not possible" (**186**,30 f.). If viewed in this light, *Angela* may be read in the end as a novel that probes into an inter-ethnic conflict but does not offer any pat solutions, much less a happy-end. What it does offer is the painful discovery by a young adult of her own racism and of the terrible guilt of her grandfather.

Teaching Points

Students tend to be fascinated by the issue of the stolen generation and usually present well-argued reports that need little, if any, supplementing. So the following tasks provide basically an alternative for those teachers who prefer a more teacher-based approach.

1. *Collect and evaluate all the information about Derek Campbell as given by himself.* (**76**,10–**77**,25)
2. *Compare this account to that given by Mrs Riley.* (**90**,11–**91**,27)
3. *What is Gracey's view of this account?* (**129**,3–11)
4. *What does Angela learn from Harry Falkirk about Derek Campbell?* (**165**,37–**168**,15)

5. *Evaluate the justification for the action given by both Mr Falkirk and Mr Malvern.* (cf. **166**,18–26; **168**,11–15; **173**,16–20; **173**,35–**174**,9)
6. *Explain and comment on Mrs Malvern's statement: "You [her husband] were determined to kill off the black man in that Campbell boy"* (**174**,15).

A thorough discussion of tasks 1–4 could yield the following results:

(Blackboard summary)

The story of Derek Campbell		
Derek's account	*Mrs Riley's account*	*Harry Falkirk's account*
– he lost his ethnic background and family	– Derek was born on a reserve full of violence and alcoholism	– half-caste kids were given a chance by the authorities
– he was given a 'white' identity	– Mr Malvern saved the boy's life	– Campbell's mother was forced to give away her son
– he received a white middle-class education	– Derek's mother voluntarily gave up the boy	
– he re-discovered his ethnic roots	– Grandfather did the right thing	
– he blames white Australian authorities for the untimely death of his mother		
	⇑ *Gracey's comment:* • the account must be wrong • it goes against Aboriginal family values	

31

As for the justification for the action as presented by Falkirk and Malvern, the following results can be expected:

(Blackboard summary)

How Derek's enforced adoption was justified

- it was official policy
- it was to give the boy the chance to develop his potential
- it was in the interest of both the boy and all Aboriginals

⇒ underlying premise: the end justifies the means

⇧
Mrs Malvern's comment:
a fundamental dislike of blacks and
white ethnocentrism were the motivating force

Note: The issue of the stolen generation is the theme of "Heart is Where the Home is" by Thea Astley in *Short Stories from Down Under* (Klettnummer 579120).

11. Seventh Teaching Unit: Angela and Jarred

Of all the relationships described in the novel, the love between Jarred and Angela comes nearest to a cliché. While Gracey and Angela undergo decisive changes in the course of the novel and, in the case of Angela, even greatly mature, Jarred remains basically the same person throughout. He is just as steady, calm and understanding at the end, after all the emotional turmoil between Angela and Gracey is over, as he was at the beginning of his relationship with Angela.

Angela meets Jarred, a third-year sports student, on the university campus. From the very beginning, he is cast in the role of the attentive, understanding adviser who even acts as a kind of agony aunt figure. When Angela talks to him about the growing estrangement between Gracey and herself, he reacts in a fashion typical of him: "'Gracey just looks a bit stirred up to me. When someone gets touchy like that, you have to leave them for a while and it will come good again in the end'" (**93**,5–7). And later he suggests to Angela: "'Can't you both ignore this Aboriginal stuff? [...] Just don't talk about it, make it a no-go area'" (**119**,25–27). Jarred thus emerges as a practical-minded, pragmatic problem-solver who not only shows understanding but is also supportive and helpful.

Even though Jarred appears to be a bit of a cliché boyfriend, there are many different facets to his character. As Gracey increasingly grows apart from Angela, he becomes the focal point in Angela's life and displays an amazing amount of sensitivity. While sitting in a fast food restaurant on their way to Sydney, it is Jarred who instinctively realizes that Gracey cannot afford to pay for a meal and unobtrusively manages to share his chips with her (**102**,23–26). And it is he who manages to persuade her to try to enter the track and field qualification runs for the Commonwealth Games and begins to coach her.

Typically enough, Jarred not only proves to be a committed coach whose optimism and can-do mentality infect Gracey so that she does qualify for the Commonwealth Games trials. More importantly, he also turns out to be able to accept Gracey on her own terms. Unlike Angela, he seems free of any form of latent racism and does not seek to impose 'white' norms on her: "'I think I can understand Gracey ... what she wants to do, what she needs right now. [...] It's up to her really, Angela, and maybe we should be helping her instead of trying to change her mind'" (150,13–17). Moreover, Jarred acts very responsibly, whereas Angela is jealous and sulky and acts stubbornly, wrongly suspecting Gracey and Jarred of having become lovers.

If one juxtaposes Angela and Jarred, Angela emerges as an immature, childish and spoiled young student, who is selfish, demanding and latently racist. Jarred, on the other hand, is supportive, good-natured and shows genuine concern and a great sense of responsibility. In terms of their relationship, Jarred's role is that of fatherly adviser, whereas Angela is the naive and childish fresher. If one wants to find fault with Moloney at all, it is his use of traditional clichés in the male-female roles in the novel.

Teaching Points

Of all the topics dealt with, the relationship between Angela and Jarred is clearly the least demanding and is therefore particularly suitable for weaker students. The teacher who wishes to follow a guided approach could make use of the tasks suggested below.

1. *Work out the characteristic features of the relationship between Angela and Jarred by examining the following passages:*

   68,19–30; **118**,16–**119**,28; **142**,29–**143**,6; **152**,34–**154**,7; **180**,34 to the end.

2. *How does Jarred deal with Gracey? Study the following passages:*

   116, 31–**118**, 15; **144**,30–**145**,25.

An extensive analysis should yield the results as shown on the next page.

(Blackboard summary)

The relationship between Angela and Jarred	
Jarred is	*Angela is*
– understanding, supportive – patient, pragmatic – tolerant, forgiving	– immature, childish – stubborn, spoiled – self-centred *but becomes* – mature, thoughtful – willing to accept Gracey
traditional male-female roles: Jarred: the reasonable, responsible, open-minded adviser Angela (*initially*): the immature, emotional, childish girl	

The discussion of task 2 should furnish the following insights:

(Blackboard summary)

Jarred's attitude towards Gracey

- he shows no kind of racism whatsoever
- he is helpful, supportive and responsible
- he accepts Gracey on her own terms

12. Worksheets and Skills Files

Worksheet I: Part One – "Schoolies"

After reading this part of the novel fill in the information on the following topics that you find important.

Angela	
Gracey	
Their friendship	
Angela's mother	
The race issue	
The importance of family ties	
Angela as a first-person narrator	

Worksheet II

While reading the novel concentrate on one of the topics below. Become an expert on it. Take notes and present your findings to the course / class.

Topics / Tasks:

1. **Angela and Gracey: the development of their friendship**
   - What is their relationship like at Hamilton College and during the beach holiday?
   - How does the relationship change after they have become university students?
   - Why does Gracey move out of the Rileys' home?
   - How can Gracey reproach Angela with having 'colonised' her?

2. **Angela as a first-person narrator**
   - At the beginning Angela thinks: "No one knew Gracey better than me" (**7,19**). What does this statement reveal about Angela?
   - How perceptive, honest or reliable are Angela's remarks and thoughts about Gracey?

3. **Gracey's growing awareness of race**
   - Why does Gracey not think and feel like an Aboriginal at the beginning?
   - When and how does her attitude change? How is this change reflected in her language?
   - What influence does Rhonda have on Gracey?

4. **The issue of the stolen generation**
   - Why was Derek Campbell taken from his mother?
   - How does he present his life with his white foster parents?
   - How does Angela react to the speeches?
   - What does Angela learn from her mother about Derek Campbell's youth?
   - Why does Angela lie to Gracey about this?
   - Why does Gracey refuse to consider Mrs Riley's version of Derek Campbell's youth?

5. **Angela and Jarred**
   - Why does Jarred become so important to Angela?
   - What role does he assume for her?

Skills File 1: How to read without a dictionary

After you have read the opening section of the novel, you know who the two protagonists are, you know something about their background, and you will have realized that Gracey may have problems in finding her place in white Anglo-Australian society. Thus you have grasped the *general outline* of the story. However, you may have difficulties with some unknown words. The following tips will help you to cope with these difficulties successfully.

Context

Very often the meaning of a word can be guessed from the context, as in the following sentence:

> *Gracey was still there though, <u>nestled into</u> the sand beside me.* (**16**,14f.)

If you think of where Angela and Gracey are, and that Angela wakes up to find Gracey close beside her, <u>nestled into</u> can only mean something like <u>lying or sitting comfortably</u> (as in a nest).

Similar German, French or Latin words

Sometimes an English word is similar to a word you know from other languages, as in the following two sentences:

1. *You spilled a bit, accidentally, then some went into the <u>ornamental</u> fig ...* (**16,** 34–**17**,1).
2. *Like it was the <u>grog</u> that made him hang himself ...* (**17**,9f.).

You know both words from Latin or German and so you can easily understand their meaning in the sentences above.

Word family

Sometimes you know a word as a noun but you have not yet come across it as a verb or adjective. If you think of the word family, you can easily understand the new word, as in the following sentence:

> *I love the way she <u>bosses</u> the blokes around ...* (**17**,31).

Getting the gist

Occasionally you are confronted with an unknown word and yet you somehow manage to understand the gist of the sentence without understanding the new word exactly, as will be the case in the following:

> ... *morning tea was set out on <u>starched</u> linen tablecloths.* (**5**,8)

As you understand *linen* and *tablecloths*, there is really no need for you to know precisely what <u>starched</u> means, but you get the gist of the scene.

If you apply these tips and think of the general outline of the novel, you will be able to read through the rest of the novel without having to consult a dictionary.

Skills File 2: Keeping a reading journal

While you are reading *Angela* you may want to take notes on what you have read and comment on it. Making notes about what you have read may help you with the following:

- *understanding the characters*
  As the characters are presented step by step your note-taking will make it easier for you to write an analysis of any of the major characters.

- *understanding the issues involved*
  As the story is narrated in chronological order your note-taking enables you to trace the development of, for example, the issue of race.

- *having information at the ready*
  Keeping a reading journal will provide you with plenty of information to refer to when discussing the novel in class.

- *reviewing your own reactions*
  If you jot down your comments on what a character does or how he or she reacts in a given situation, you will enrich your own reading experience and will have these comments at your disposal for discussions in class.

A sensible way of keeping track of what is going on is to note down information under the following headings:

- <u>Who?</u>   (= Which character is described? How does he or she change/develop?)
- <u>What?</u>   (= What problem/issue is dealt with?)
- <u>Where?</u> (= Where does the scene take place? What is the significance of the setting?)
- <u>When?</u>   (= Are there any time references?)
- <u>How?</u>   (= Is the action presented as a dialogue, reported thought or as a description by the narrator?)

There is no need for you to stop reading after each chapter in order to take notes. Simply write up your reading journal whenever you feel you have read enough.
Mark those passages in your journal that you think might interest the other students and present them to the course/class.

Skills File 3: Writing a (video) screenplay

1. Re-read again quietly to yourself the scene on Bondi Beach between Angela and Gracey ("Bankstown", Section 5, **125**,20–**129**,16).[1]

2. Imagine you want to film this scene. Write the script/screenplay for it, which should include the following points:
   - what the scenery should be like;
   - how you would use the camera;
   - how Angela and Gracey should look and speak;
   - how facial expressions and body language should emphasize what is being said;
   - the dialogue between the two girls.

3. Before you start, read the following words and expressions. They will help you when you think about the camera work.
   - *to focus on*: to point the camera at
   - *long shot*: this shows the entire setting
   - *full shot*: this shows all of the subject and the immediate surroundings
   - *close-up*: the camera is very close to the subject
   - *detail-shot*: the camera shows us a detail of a subject or an object
   - *eye-level angle*: the camera is at the same level as the actor's eyes
   - *over-the-shoulder shot*: the camera is placed behind one speaker and focuses on the dialogue partner
   - *high-angle shot*: the camera looks down on a subject
   - *low-angle shot*: the camera is positioned below a subject or object
   - *to tilt up or down*: to move (the camera) up or down along a vertical plane
   - *to pan/panning shot*: the camera swings around along a horizontal plane.

---

[1] Alternatively, you may choose another scene of your own liking.

13. Post-reading Activities

The various activities suggested below specify some of the ideas outlined in Chapter 2, "Die didaktische Konzeption".

a) *Reviewing your own reading experience*

If you have kept a reading journal, now could be the time to have another look at your notes and comments on a given scene, action etc. How do you now view what you put down several weeks ago?
If you have a different view of the passage/scene now, what has changed your opinion?
Find a partner and discuss your individual reading of the book.

b) *Writing a (video) screenplay*

Find a suitable scene from the novel and draft a scene for a screenplay. You can use Skills File 3. Present your ideas to the course/class and discuss them.

c) *Writing your own book review*

Write a review of *Angela*. Present a short summary of the novel, evaluate it critically by dealing with one or two points in a more detailed way, and finish your review with a well-argued recommendation either to read the book as soon as possible or not to spend any time on it at all. (You can compare your review with the one printed in the Student's Book, **186–187**.)

d) *Chatting on the internet*

Try to get in touch with Australian or other foreign readers on the internet and exchange your views on the novel. Inform your course about interesting ideas you've heard from your chatting partners.

14. Working with the Additional Texts

I. The Review (SB 186–187)

Tasks

1. *Collect all the words and phrases that express either* praise *or* criticism *of the novel.*
2. *How does the writer develop* her line of argument?
3. *What do you make of the writer's remark:* "I feel that as an exploration of a social issue, the novel needed to have Gracey older so that her attitude would've been more realistic"?
4. *Write a* letter to the editor *in which you develop your own views on the novel as well as comment on the review by Pip Masson-Naake.*

The purpose of the review is primarily functional, i.e. it is meant to stimulate a final student-centred assessment of the novel. The review should be read and prepared at home while tasks 1 and 2 should be a written assignment.

1. The following points could be collected on the board:

judgements on the novel	
praise	*criticism*
– well-told story – impartial presentation of a political issue – brilliant attempt to present the issue of the stolen generation to young readers – brilliantly written novel, deep understanding of human emotions	– no real insight into lives of young Aborigines today – Gracey's racial awakening happens too fast, and is not very convincing – the issue of the stolen generation doesn't interest the younger generation – the novel doesn't reach its intended audience: black and white adolescents

2. The writer's *line of argument* can be summarised as follows:
   - she summarises the plot of the novel
   - she emphasizes the writer's balanced view of race relations and praises his non-escapist stance
   - she questions the writer's depiction of Gracey's development
   - she briefly outlines the political interests of contemporary Aboriginal youth
   - she assesses the novel in a twofold way: she praises Moloney's depiction of character, but she criticises his depiction of the race issue

3. Students are expected to deal with the writer's remark by either supporting it with additional reasons presented by them or by arguing against it. They should become aware of the fact that review writing is influenced by the *zeitgeist*, by cultural norms and values, and above all by one's own reading experience.

4. In their *letter to the editor* the students are required to employ an argumentative discourse, to take up the writer's double-edged assessment and to unfold their own point of view in a coherent line of argument.

II. The Speech (SB 188–190)

1. *How has Keating structured his address?*
2. *Examine his line of argument: consider assertions, value judgements, his projection of a vision etc.*
3. *What view does the speaker hold of Aboriginal history?*
4. *How does he try to win the support of his audience for the reconciliation process?*

The speech should be read and prepared at home; tasks 1 and 2 can be a written assignment.
A thorough discussion of all four tasks should yield the results presented on the following pages.

1. (Blackboard summary)

Structure of address

- Part I (**188**,1–14): the speaker views the treatment of the Aborigines as a test of Australian social democracy
- Part II (**188**,15–**189**,13): he reviews Australian history and stresses the need for a process of reconciliation
- Part III (189,14–190,3): he acknowledges the wrongs done to the indigenous population by white Australians and their failure to right these wrongs
- Part IV (**190**,3–12): he appeals to the emotions of his white listeners
- Part V (**190**,13–22): he acknowledges the debt to the Aborigines and projects his belief in a mutually better future

---

2. *Major elements in Keating's line of argument*
    - continuous use of 'failed'/'failure' to stress the injustices and crimes committed by Anglo-Australians in their dealings with the Aborigines
    - repeated use of 'test' to stress the significance of the process
    - use of assertions (**188**,3; **188**,11; **188**,24–25; **189**,3–4; **189**,24–25) emphasising the singularity of the situation and the need for change
    - use of value judgements (**188**,17–18; **189**,14; **189**,31–33) to underline the collective guilt of past generations of white Australians
    - projection of a better future (**188**,27–**189**,3; **190**,13–22) to emphasize his vision of reconciliation and to stress the changes under way.

3. (Blackboard summary)

Keating's view of Aboriginal history

- he points out the wrongs done to the Aborigines
- Aboriginal history is contrasted with the reasons for white and Asian immigration
- Aboriginal history is closely linked to the white settlers' history
- Aboriginal history was suppressed/destroyed
- he points out the strength of Aboriginal culture and praises its contribution to Australian life.

4. *How does he try to win the support of the audience for the reconciliation process?*
Keating uses several rhetorical devices to raise people's consciousness of the problem and to mobilise them to take action in the reconciliation process.

He frequently uses imperatives, which shows that he wants to appeal directly to the listeners because he aims to get them to think about what he has said and act on it.

He also uses the inclusive 'we', which should rouse a sense of responsibility as well as a feeling of solidarity or community between Anglo-Australians and the indigenous population. This also shows that he includes himself in the wrongdoings of the white Australian population and their collective guilt.

Within his enumeration of wrongs done to the Aboriginals in lines 26 of page 189 to line 3 of page 190 a syntactic parallelism between the sentences can be noticed, which should underline that not one of the deeds was justified, they are all "morally indefensible" (**189**,14).

Keating's repeated requests to 'imagine' in lines 4 to 12 of page 190 gradually intensify and have their climax in the sentence: "Imagine if our spiritual life was denied and ridiculed" (**190**,11–12). This reflects Keating's intention of gaining the audience's support as he points out the ultimate wrong.

His repeated use of the 'going-to' future as well as the anaphoric repetitions finally signal the speaker's conviction that the process leading to his vision of the future has just started but will inevitably lead to a better future.

III. Students' Questions on *Angela* (SB **191–192**)

The questions and answers can easily be used for different purposes such as

- a starting point for re-thinking some of one's own ideas about the novel
- a basis for internet chats with students in Germany or Australia
- an incentive to start an e-mail correspondence with the author.

15. Suggested Tests

I. 11th Form: Gracey at Hamilton College

The following excerpt is from Moloney's novel Gracey *(1994). It describes a scene during a ballnight at Hamilton College and is narrated by Gracey.*

"Had to get his address," Matthew explained as he returned to the group. "My dear old mother made me promise. She wants a picture of me in this monkey suit with the young lady who invited me along. And I always do what my mother asks," he added to get a laugh. "She's
5 going to freak out, of course."
"Why?" Angela asked him.
"Because she'll see that Grace is Aboriginal, that's why. She'll just about faint."
He turned directly towards me now, to explain more personally.
10 "She's been going on about what a nice girl you sounded on the phone. It will teach her a lesson."
"What do you mean?" I asked.
His tone was as friendly and intimate as ever, but I was confused. Was he insulting me now, after all this? His face was too open, too
15 likeable. No, he was explaining something to me, something that meant a lot to him.
He went on, "I mean that my mother, terrific person that she is, thinks that all Aborigines are useless drunks. So when she sees this picture of you and me, she'll get a real shock."
20 He turned back to the rest of the group then, eager to have them understand as well. "She'll see that Grace is exactly the same as everyone else here tonight. Maybe she'll learn something from that. That unless you see the colour of the skin, you can't tell the difference. And that's the whole point. There isn't any difference between Grace
25 and you, Angela, or any of the girls here tonight." He stopped there, pleased with his little speech and keen to see the reactions of the others.
"But there is a difference," I said. "Angela and the others are white girls and I'm not. I'm an Aborigine."
30 "But you're not an Aborigine like most people think of them, Grace," Matthew said. "You ask most people to describe an Aborigine

and they'll answer like my mother. I'll bet there's not a person here tonight who's thought of you as Aboriginal. That photograph's going to prove something to my mother, I can guarantee it."

As the night drew to a close we moved back inside then to join in the whirl. The sober little discussion in the foyer was swept away in the noise and movement and I'm sure that for the others, it was forgotten.

But I couldn't forget. In that final half-hour we swapped partners and gathered in small groups arm-in-arm around the dance floor, and at one stage I found myself alone at the edge, watching the others. I was there for no more than a minute, before I was claimed by a wildly laughing semicircle of friends with Angela leading them in a high-kick routine like a line of chorus girls. But I was alone long enough to take in all those I knew and liked and called my friends, and to hear Matthew's words again: *"You're no different from the rest of the girls, Grace."*

Had he said it in those words? That was how I heard it at that moment. And it was true. I was no different – not as far as these friends were concerned. In the two-and-a-half years I had been at Hamilton College, I had learned to be exactly like the other girls and they accepted me completely because of it. They didn't think of me as an Aborigine any more. It was true.

And then and there a question whirled out of the dance floor and started to nag at me. *"So, Grace,"* it asked. *"Are you an Aborigine any more? Are you, are you?"*

And then the line of girls swept up and gathered me in and the moment was gone in all but my memory.

625 words

From *Gracey* by James Moloney, St. Lucia: Queensland University Press, 1994, pp. 72–74. Printed by permission of the University of Queensland Press.

Tasks

1. Outline Matthew's attitude towards Aborigines and set it against Gracey's self-awareness as a black.

2. Analyse how the narrative perspective reflects Gracey's state of mind.

3. Write a diary entry in which, years later, Gracey thinks about her ethnic self-awareness when she was at Hamilton College.

Results to be expected

1. Matthew clearly uses Gracey as an instrument to teach his racist mother a lesson. She seems to have very definite stereotyped and prejudiced notions about Aborigines, whom she considers to be 'useless drunks'.
   At first glance, Matthew seems to be a liberal-minded, non-racist white boy. A careful reading of his arguments does reveal, however, his latent racist attitude. Similar to Angela, Matthew thinks of Gracey only as a well-adjusted, assimilated girl: "'Grace is exactly the same as everyone else here tonight'". What he fails to perceive is Gracey's ethnicity, what he does perceive is his idea of an Aborigine. Therefore he does not accept Gracey on her own terms, as an Aboriginal.
   Initially, Gracey feels confused and intimidated by Matthew's blunt words and is wondering if he is insulting her. His statement, quoted above, occupies her mind throughout the whole evening and makes her think about who she really is. When she asks herself, "Are you an Aborigine any more?", we notice that she has started to wonder about her identity as a black.

2. The novel is narrated by Gracey, so the mode of narration is that of an adolescent first-person narrator who is also a participant in the action. Gracey has not yet been confronted with racial problems or severe forms of discrimination, and she has not yet started to question the role ascribed to her by her 'white' surroundings. As readers, we gain insight into a still innocent mind which does not grasp the hidden racism inherent in Matthew's remarks.
   The thoughts presented to us show her to have little ethnic self-awareness. However, Matthew's words do leave her wondering about her own identity, as the repetition of her question indicates. In terms of racial awareness her state of mind may be characterized as expressing the beginning of a slow ethnic awakening.

3. Here the students should write from the point of view of a matured Gracey who is well aware of her own ethnicity and of both white racism and racism in reverse by blacks. Students might outline her development from an assimilated boarding school pupil to an independent-minded, self-assured young woman. They are also expected to take into consideration the form and style of diary-writing, i.e. their writing should be personal, not too matter-of-fact, and include emotional aspects as well.

II. 12th/13th Form: Prime Minister John Howard's Address to Corroboree 2000

This is the text of the speech which Prime Minister John Howard made to Corroboree 2000, the opening ceremony for National Reconciliation Week.

First, may I acknowledge that I speak to you on the traditional lands of the Eora people. I pay my respects to them and thank them for the warmth of their welcome. [...]
   I think all of us recognise the debt we owe to the tremendous hard
5 work of the Council for Aboriginal Reconciliation over the last ten years. [...] It has been a long journey and I know it has been difficult. I know there have been areas of disagreement and it is naive of any of us to pretend that some do not remain. But let all of us try this weekend, and for my part I pledge that I will in what I say, to focus on
10 those things that unite us and bind us together as Australians, in the cause of healing the wounds and the divisions of the past and of moving forward in a united and harmonious fashion.
   It is quite impossible for anyone to attend a gathering such as this without being captured and moved by its symbolism and the speciality
15 of the occasion. I think it is an expression of a desire of all Australians to go forward, not to forget or ignore or fail to express sorrow or regret for the pain of the past. It is impossible to understand the difficulty and the reality of today and to move forward effectively, without understanding and acknowledging the pain that was inflicted by the
20 injustices of the past. And it is not possible, it is not possible for any of us, to reflect upon the desirability of moving forward without acknowledging the impact that European civilisation had on the indigenous people of this country and the cultures of the indigenous people.
25   This weekend is an occasion for all Australians to honour the contribution of the indigenous people of Australia to the life of this country. It is an occasion to honour the special character of their cultures. It is an occasion to thank them for the generosity of their spirit, and it is an occasion to recognise the richness that their cultures
30 bring to modern Australian life.
   As the Council's declaration says, we are a nation of many origins. We are a nation of many cultures, and the 60,000 years of human habitation which has produced the cultures of the indigenous people

has so much to offer to all of us. And we can together respect the speciality of those cultures and also draw tremendous inspiration from what we have built together. To recognise and acknowledge and express regret for the pain of the mistakes and the injustices of the past, but also, hopefully, my friends, to draw some inspiration from what we have achieved together.

And so much of what the Council has endeavoured to do has been to focus on those things that do keep us together, those things that we can draw inspiration in common. So my fellow Australians, this is an occasion, it is a weekend to frankly acknowledge the tragedies and sadness and the pain and the hurt and the cruelty of the past. To accept the ongoing trauma of that. But it is also, my friends, an occasion to celebrate and rejoice in those things that we have achieved together.

And, very importantly, it is an occasion for all of us to resolve to continue the process of reconciliation. As the Council so rightly said in its document, there are many paths to reconciliation, but ultimately they reach one destination. And each of us brings our own perspective to the process of reconciliation, and the one requirement that we should bring to that is the sincerity of the view that we hold on how reconciliation might be achieved.

Reconciliation will mean different things to different people. There is a spiritual component to reconciliation just as there is a practical component to it. And you cannot achieve reconciliation without acknowledging, as I do and as the Government I lead does, the self-evident fact that the indigenous peoples of Australia are the most profoundly disadvantaged within our communities. And part of the process of reconciliation is to adopt practical measures to address that disadvantage. [...]

The Government does remain firmly committed to the ongoing process of reconciliation. We may have differences as to how that may be achieved, we may have [different] points of departure, but the common goal of achieving reconciliation is very sincerely held by all members of the Government. And it will be our desire and our wish to support and help and assist any ongoing reconciliation trust that emerges independent of government and [that] is an expression of the desire of all of the Australian people to continue the process of reconciliation. [...]

Thank you. *790 words*

Source: www.dpmc.gov.au

Annotations

Corroboree (*AustrE*): *usu.* an Aboriginal ceremony of sacred or festive character; *here:* the March for Reconciliation across Sydney Harbour Bridge on March 27, 2000
- 2 **Eora**: Aboriginal people living in the Sydney region
- 5 **Council for Aboriginal Reconciliation**: established in 1991 to work towards the reconciliation of indigenous and non-indigenous Australians
- 9 **to pledge:** to promise solemnly
- 40 **to endeavour:** to try very hard
- 45 **ongoing:** continuing
- 48 **to resolve:** to make a firm decision to do s.th.

Tasks

1. What information is given in the address about the situation of the Aboriginals in the past and in the present?
2. Examine the rhetorical devices which Prime Minister Howard employs in his speech to gain the sympathy and support of his listeners.
3. If you compare this address to Paul Keating's Redfern Speech (**188–190**), which do you find more interesting or informative as regards the Aboriginals' place in Australian society?

Results to be expected

1. The speaker begins by characterising efforts to achieve reconciliation as a long and difficult journey and stresses the necessity of "healing wounds". He acknowledges in general terms the "pain of the past" and "the injustices" done to the Aboriginal people. He places these injustices into the context of Australia's colonial history and the impact European civilization had on the life and cultures of the Aboriginal population.
He then praises the contributions of these people to Australian life and history, and notes the progress that has been achieved so far.
He deplores once more the wrongs of the past and calls on his listeners to continue to work towards reconciliation. The Prime Minister points out that the Aborigines of today are still the "most profoundly disadvantaged" group within Australian society and he promises that his government will take measures to improve that situation. He closes his address by pledging the continuing support of his government to the process of reconciliation.

2. The overall strategy underlying the Prime Minister's address is to emphasize the need for togetherness and consensus within Australian society. He begins by paying his respects to the Aboriginal people, thus trying to gain their good will. By comparing the present state of race relations to a journey he introduces two major ideas that run as a leitmotif through his speech. His reference to a journey suggests progress and, at the same time, a destination still to be reached. He briefly juxtaposes the past ("wounds") with a vision of the future ("moving forward in a united and harmonious fashion"). The technique of contrasting past and future is also the dominating device in the third paragraph (lines 13–24). Here the speaker acknowledges that to move forward in race relations is to admit the wrongs of the past. Significantly, he is very imprecise when dealing with past history, as he uses such vague and emotionally charged words as "pain", "tragedy" or "trauma".
The speaker tries again and again to evoke a feeling of unity and togetherness by frequently using the inclusive "we" or the possessive determiner "our". His appeal to his listeners' national pride is clearly meant to cut across racial and ethnic differences: "We are a nation of many origins".
John Howard then draws again on the motif of the journey, emphasizing that, regardless of differences of opinion, "all paths"

will finally lead to "one destination," i.e. the reconciliation of indigenous and non-indigenous Australians.

3. Paul Keating's Redfern Speech was held eight years before John Horward's. Students should notice major differences as regards the speakers' attitudes towards the Aborigines, and assess the rhetorical impact of the second address. One major difference refers to the fact that Keating is much more outspoken as regards the injustices done to the Aborigines. He enumerates precisely the crimes committed against the indigenous people and speaks of the moral failure of the Anglo-Australians. Howard, on the other hand, plays down these crimes by speaking of "pain", "cruelty" or "sadness". This flowery, even melodramatic, wording stops short of acknowledging the white man's guilt.

Another difference refers to the speed with which the reconciliation is to come about. In 1992 Keating closed his speech on the optimistic note: "I am confident that we will succeed in this decade". Eight years later Prime Minister Howard uses the metaphor of a "journey" to gloss over the halting progress in race relations.

Students might also argue that Keating's speech seems more sincere, whereas Howard tends to be vague and non-committal.

Useful Internet Addresses

I. General

Australian Academy of Science: www.science.org.au/
Australian Broadcasting Corporation: www.abc.net.au/
Australian Embassy in Germany: www.australian-embassy.de
Australian Government, science and tourism: www.dist.gov.au
Australian literature resources on the internet:
www.nla.gov.au/oz/litsites.html
Australian places:
www.monash.edu.au/ncas/multimedia/gazetteer/
Australisches Studiencenter Universität Potsdam:
www.australiacentre.org.

II. Australian newspapers

Australian newspapers index:
www.compucan.com/Newsstand/australian-newspapers.htm
The Australian internet menu's guide to Australian newspapers:
www.maldivesculture.com/
Australian and New Zealand newspapers – virtual library:
www.broadcast-live.com/newspapers/australian.html
Australian newspapers on the internet:
www.nla.gov.au/oz/npapers.html

or

On-line archives: www.smh.com.au
www.theage.com.au
www.theaustralian.com.au

III. Government

Federal Government of Australia: www.fed.gov.au
New South Wales: www.nsw.gov.au
Northern Territory: www.nt.gov.au
Queensland: www.qld.gov.au
South Australia: www.sa.gov.au
Victoria: www.vic.gov.au
Western Australia: www.wa.gov.au

IV. Aboriginal issues

www.atsia.com.au
- Media center
- Latest media releases, speeches and reports
- Indigenous fact sheets
- Separated children
- Direct link to www.reconciliation.org.au

www.reconciliation.org.au
- Key speeches and media releases
- Corroboree 2000

www. dpmc.gov.au
- Office of indigenous policy
- Minister for Aboriginal and Torres Strait Islanders Affairs
- Council for Aboriginal Reconciliation
- Quick search for documents under the headword 'separated children' (219 documents found)
- Quick search for speeches under the headword 'political speeches'
- Direct link to www.pm.gov.au (Prime Minister)

www.pm.gov.au
- News room
- Speeches

V. James Moloney

www.home.gil.com.au

VI. Internet chats

An easy starting point is: www.englisch.schule.de